The Library of the Thirteen Colonies and the Lost Colony™

Roanoke: The Lost Colony

Brooke Coleman

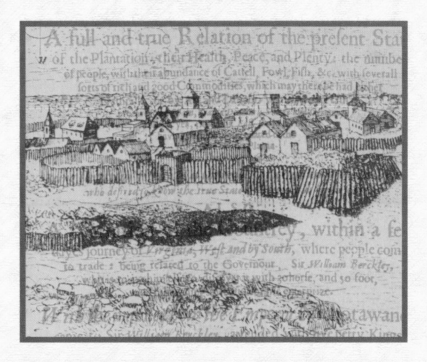

The Rosen Publishing Group's
PowerKids Press™
New York

To Both My Daniels

Published in 2000 by The Rosen Publishing Group, Inc.
29 East 21st Street, New York, NY 10010

Photo Credits: p. 1 © Corbis-Bettmann; p. 4 © New York Public Library, New York/ET Archive/London/ SuperStock, © SuperStock, © Archive Photos; p. 7 © Corbis-Bettmann; p. 8 © SuperStock; p. 11 © SuperStock; p. 12 © The Bettmann Archive; p. 15 © Corbis-Bettmann; p. 16 © SuperStock; p. 19 © Corbis-Bettmann; p. 20 © SuperStock; p. 22 © The Lost Colony, Roanoke Island, NC

First Edition

Book Design: Andrea Levy

Coleman, Brooke.
      Roanoke: The Lost Colony / by Brooke Coleman.
            p.   cm.—(The thirteen colonies and the Lost Colony series)
      Includes index.
      Summary: Describes the two attempts by English colonists to establish a settlement on Roanoke Island at the end of the 16th century.
      ISBN 0-8239-5473-0
      1. Roanoke Colony—Juvenile literature. 2. Roanoke Island (N.C.)—History—Juvenile literature. [1. Roanoke Colony.]
      I. Title. II. Series
      F229.C66 1999
      975.6'175—dc21   98-32366
                                                                            CIP
                                                                            AC

Manufactured in the United States of America

Contents

CHAWA

NOROGOKI

VIRGINIA

Ranushousoo

M.ongoack

Ohanoock

the Ioanne With
ore Theodoro
Qui et excud

Moratuc

ECO

Tanequomuc
Metocuicum

Catokinge

TAN

Waratan

Mascoming

Skicoak

Aguscogoc

Chep

Mequopen

Paquippe

Tramasquecoock

Pomeiock

Pasquenoke

Wokokon

Dasamonquepeuc

Roanoac

Trinety harb

Croatoan

Hatorask

Paquiwoc

Scala leucarum. 25

10 15 20 25

SEPT

ORIENS

The New World

After Christopher Columbus brought news of the New World back to Europe in 1492, a race started among the nations of Europe. France, Spain, England, and other

Manteo, an Indian from America, returned to England with the explorers. Many people in England, including the Queen, were eager to meet Native Americans. Manteo enjoyed visiting England, and learned to speak English quickly.

nations sent **explorers** to the New World, later called America. They hoped to get gold for their countries. England's Queen Elizabeth wanted more than gold. She wanted an English **colony** in America. In 1584, she gave Sir Walter Raleigh a **patent**, which gave him the right to **claim** land for England. His first claim was for a large part of the East Coast in America. He called that land Virginia. Raleigh returned to England to report on the new land. A friendly local Indian named Manteo agreed to come to England, too.

Explorers like Christopher Columbus sailed in search of land and gold.

5

The First Try at Starting a Colony

Sir Walter Raleigh sent his cousin Sir Richard Grenville, a famous naval **commander**, to America in 1585. Grenville's job was to find a good place for English **settlers** to live. Manteo, the helpful Indian Raleigh had met on the first **expedition**, traveled with Grenville. Manteo helped pick Roanoke Island as the place for the English colony. The soil was not the best for growing crops, but Roanoke was close to Manteo and his friendly tribe of **Croatoan** Indians, who lived on a nearby island. In 1585, at the time of the second expedition, Grenville left about 100 men, including artist John White, to start an English colony at Roanoke. Grenville returned to England.

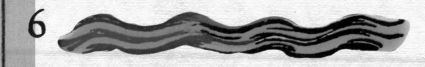

Here is one of the paintings John White, the artist, did of Roanoke Island. ▶

Dasamonquepeuc

WE

Roanoac

Hatorask

Trinety harbor

Hard Times in Roanoke

The Roanoke settlers were soldiers, not farmers. Even with help from Manteo and his family, they could not grow all the food they needed. Other nearby tribes didn't trust the settlers. Without enough help to grow food, the settlers had to struggle to **survive**.

Founding an English colony in America began to seem like a bad idea. When the great English **navigator** Sir Francis Drake visited Roanoke during a voyage only a few months later, the soldiers decided to go back to England with him.

Sir Walter Raleigh realized that one of the reasons the first colony failed was that the men missed their families. On the next trip, he made sure women and children went along.

Some Native Americans did not trust white people. White people were taking over land that the Indians had lived on for hundreds of years. They also brought strange diseases, which killed Native Americans.

Another Try

A few brave and hopeful people in England still thought America would be a wonderful place to start a colony. This next attempt would be different. For the first time, whole families, not just soldiers or explorers, went to live in America. In May 1587, a group of 114 men, women, and children went to America.

They left behind friends and many of their belongings. Some people went because they couldn't find work in England. Others went to America in hopes of starting businesses or farms that could make them rich.

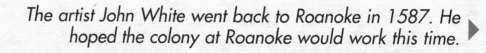

The artist John White went back to Roanoke in 1587. He hoped the colony at Roanoke would work this time. ▶

Settling In

The second group of English settlers arrived in Roanoke in July 1587. John White, the artist, was the group's leader. He was going to be the colony's new **governor**. Soon afterward Virginia Dare was born. She was the first English person born in America. Her parents named her after the new place that had become their home, but many **colonists** thought that Virginia didn't feel like home. They didn't have enough **supplies** to build the houses or grow the crops they knew they would need that winter. They asked their governor, John White, to return to England for seeds, clothing, and tools. White didn't want to leave Virginia Dare, who was his granddaughter, and the other colonists. He agreed to go, but hoped to be back soon.

◀ *Here is a picture of what one artist thinks Virginia Dare would have looked like as a grown-up.*

White Is Delayed

In 1587, John White returned to England and gathered food, clothing, and tools to take back to the colonists in Roanoke. He even found twelve more colonists who wanted to go to America. Some of them were related to people already in Roanoke. Unfortunately, when White's ship was sailing back to America, a French ship attacked it and stole all the supplies. White had to go back to England and try again.

Ocean travel could be dangerous. Ships sailing for different countries might get into fights. ▶

Trapped by War

By 1588, it had been almost a year since John White had left the colonists on Roanoke Island. He probably hoped that Manteo was helping them get through the winter without being too cold, afraid, and hungry. Still more time would go by before he could return to Roanoke. England went to war with Spain, and all of England's ships were needed to fight. White couldn't get back to Roanoke until the war ended. He was very worried about the colonists. White finally made it back to Roanoke in 1590.

◀ *English ships were needed for fighting the war.*
No ships were left to go to the colonies.

The Colonists Are Gone!

When John White returned to Roanoke he found a very upsetting sight. The town where the colonists had lived was **deserted**. Everyone was gone. White couldn't tell if the colonists had moved with all their things to a better place, or whether they had been killed by Indians, disease, or the cold. The only message they left was the word CROATOAN carved on a tree. John White tried to look for them on nearby Croatoan Island but couldn't get there because of terrible storms. He never made it to the island. He returned to England and never saw his family again.

When White came back to Roanoke, he was glad to see smoke from the colonists' cooking fires. After landing, he saw that the smoke came instead from brush fires started by lightning.

John White was not sure what the clue CROATOAN meant. ▶

The Mystery of the Lost Colony

What happened to America's first English colony? We will never know for sure. In the years to come, many explorers visited the islands of Roanoke and Croatoan, but no one ever found the colonists. Some might have decided to live with the Indians, because they thought they had been **abandoned**. Others might have moved north in search of better land. If they did settle further north, they were probably killed by the Powhatan Indians or the severe winter.

Some people believe that **descendants** of the "lost colony" of Roanoke are still alive today. They think the colonists were taken in by Manteo's tribe and family, the Croatoan Indians. Perhaps the colonists married some of them and had children who grew up as American Indians.

◀ *Some people think friendly Indian tribes helped the Roanoke settlers. Other people think unfriendly tribes may have harmed them.*

Roanoke Remembered

The mystery of the lost colony has never been solved, but it has not been forgotten either. On Roanoke Island, off the coast of today's North Carolina, a play called "The Lost Colony" has been running for over 62 summers. The play is **performed** outdoors by a cast of over 100 people. The cast usually includes local **residents**, college students, and some **professional** actors. You can call (252) 473-3414 in May for tickets to a **theatrical** trip back in time to the Lost Colony!

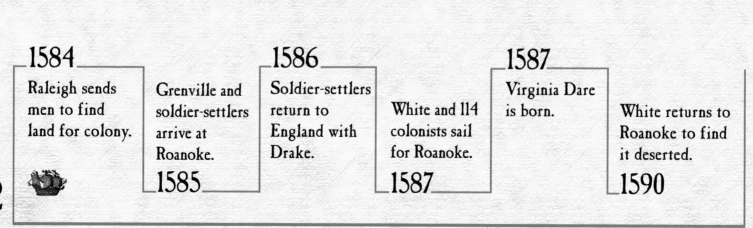

1584		**1586**		**1587**	
Raleigh sends men to find land for colony.	Grenville and soldier-settlers arrive at Roanoke.	Soldier-settlers return to England with Drake.	White and 114 colonists sail for Roanoke.	Virginia Dare is born.	White returns to Roanoke to find it deserted.
	1585		**1587**		**1590**

Glossary

abandoned (uh-BAN-dund) To be left alone with no help forever.

claim (KLAYM) To take something and say that it belongs to the person who took it.

colonist (KAH-luh-nist) Someone who lives in a colony.

colony (KAH-luh-nee) An area in a new country where a large group of people move, who are still ruled by the leaders and laws of their old country.

commander (kuh-MAN-dur) A ship's officer just below the rank of captain.

Croatoan (kroh-uh-TOH-in) A friendly Native American tribe of Croatoan Island.

descendants (dih-SEN-dintz) People born of a certain family or group.

deserted (dih-ZUR-tid) When people have left a place forever.

expedition (EK-spuh-DIH-shun) A trip people take to find out more about something.

explorer (ik-SPLOR-er) A person who travels to different places to learn more about them.

founded (FOWN-did) Established, or started something.

governor (GUH-vuh-nur) An official that is put in charge of a colony by a king or queen.

navigator (NA-vuh-gay-tur) An explorer of the seas.

patent (PA-tint) Official document that gives someone the right to claim and be in charge of an area of land.

perform (pur-FORM) To present or act out.

professional (proh-FEH-shuh-nul) Someone who gets paid to do something, such as act.

resident (REH-zih-dent) Someone who lives in a place.

settlers (SEH-tuh-lurz) People who move to a new land to live.

supplies (suh-PLYZ) Things that people need to live, like food, clothing, and tools.

survive (sur-VYV) To stay alive.

theatrical (thee-ah-tri-kul) Having to do with theater or putting on a play.

Index

Web Sites:

You can learn more about the lost colony of Roanoke on the Internet. Check out this Web site: http://www.kidinfo.com/American_History/Colonization_Roanoke.html